Country Piano Easter Celebration

by Darrell Archer

WWW.MELBAY.COM

PREFACE

When you are playing a prelude and offertory or for a special concert event, it is obvious to all that sometimes the congregation gets "swept away" and becomes intensely involved in the spirit of the moment when one of their favorite songs is being presented. Almost everyone notices that many members of the congregation spontaneously begin to tap their feet, hum or sing along, or even start to clap their hands in response to the more rhythmic songs.

The Easter season in particular is a time of great joy and celebration for the Christian believer as they hear the messages of hope, resurrection and redemption conveyed through the medium of music.

Here is a piano collection that presents the thrill and excitement of the Easter message through some creative and interesting keyboard arrangements composed in the country gospel style. Chord symbols have been included so that rhythm players can be included and also as an aid to those pianists who have improvisational capabilities.

While all of the songs in this collection communicate the good news of the gospel, some of the arrangements are more subdued and reflective and others are more energetic and upbeat. Hopefully all of the songs herein will bring pleasure to performers and listeners alike and will bring everyone involved closer to our Savior and all to a deeper appreciation of His life, sacrifice and redeeming work. May God richly bless you in your ministry as you play to His glory.

Table of Contents

Kneel at the Cross

Charles E. Moody
Arr. Darrell V. Archer

9
(8va)
B♭
B♭°7
B♭/F
B♭
B♭/F
Gm
C7
Gm7
C7
Cm
Cm7
F
F7
cresc.
13
B♭
B♭/F
B♭
E♭
mf
B♭
B♭/D
B♭/F
B♭
F7
F7/C
B♭
F7

17
B♭
B♭7/F
B♭9
2nd time to 𝄌
E♭
A♭9
B♭/F
Cm7
F7
B♭
E♭
B♭/D
A♭6
21
G
f
B7+
C
C/E
C/G
C
G
G6/D
G
G/D
3
dim.

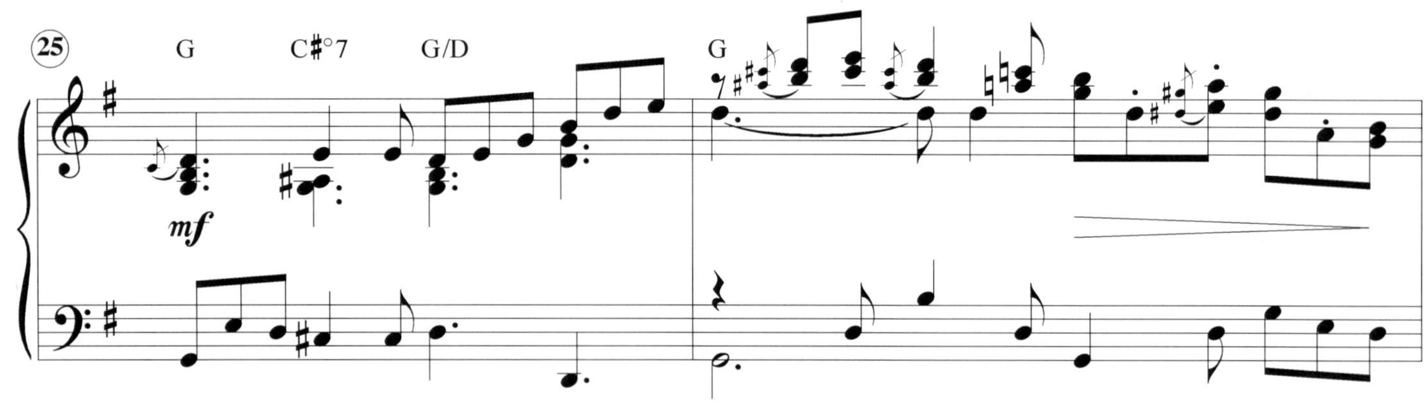
25
G
C#°7
G/D
G
mf

A
A9
A7
Am
Am7
F7
D.S. al CODA
mp
cresc.

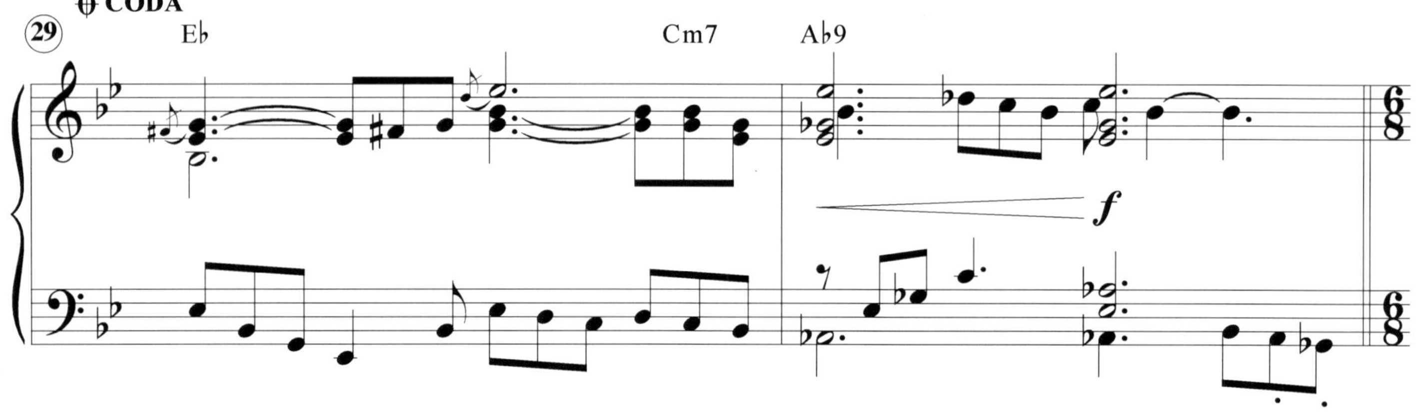
CODA
29
E♭
Cm7
A♭9
f

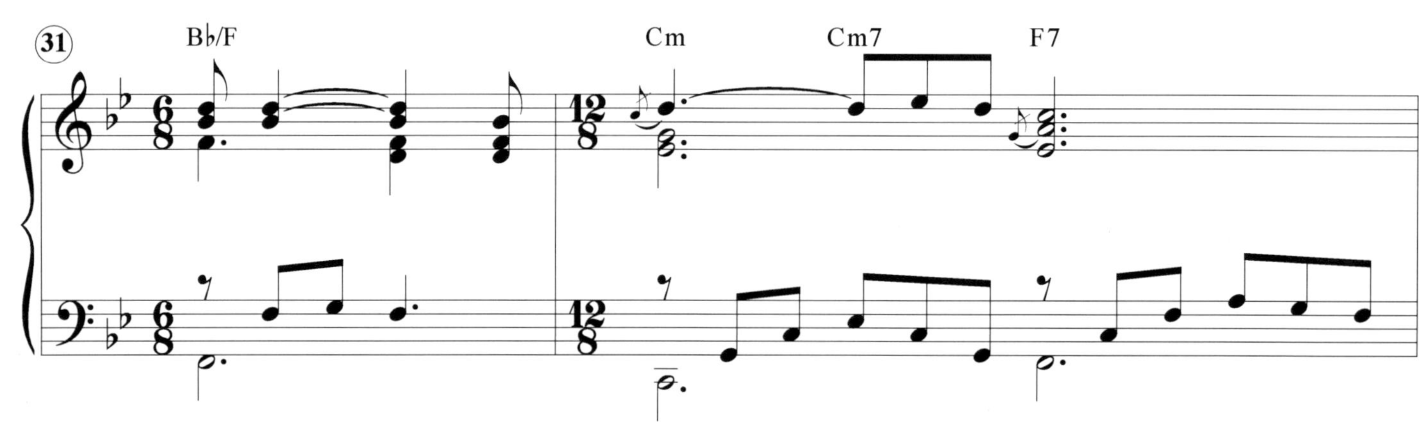
31
B♭/F
Cm
Cm7
F7

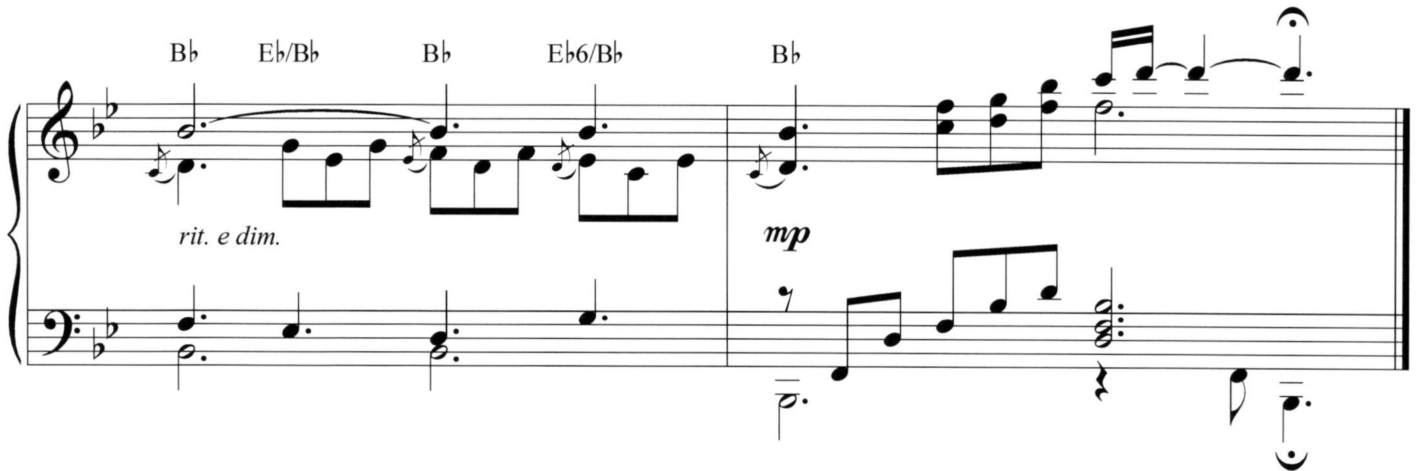

He is not here, but He has risen.

Remember how He spoke to you while He was still in Galilee,
saying that the Son of Man must be delivered into the hands of sinful men,
and be crucified, and the third day rise again.

Luke: 24:6, 7

Beneath the Cross of Jesus

Elizabeth C. Clephane

Frederick C. Maker
Arr. Darrell V. Archer

Reverently (♩ = 70)

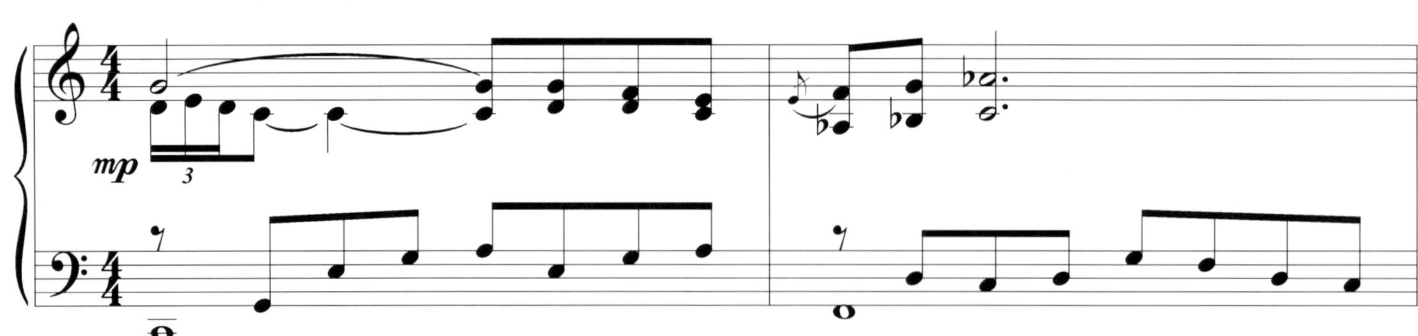

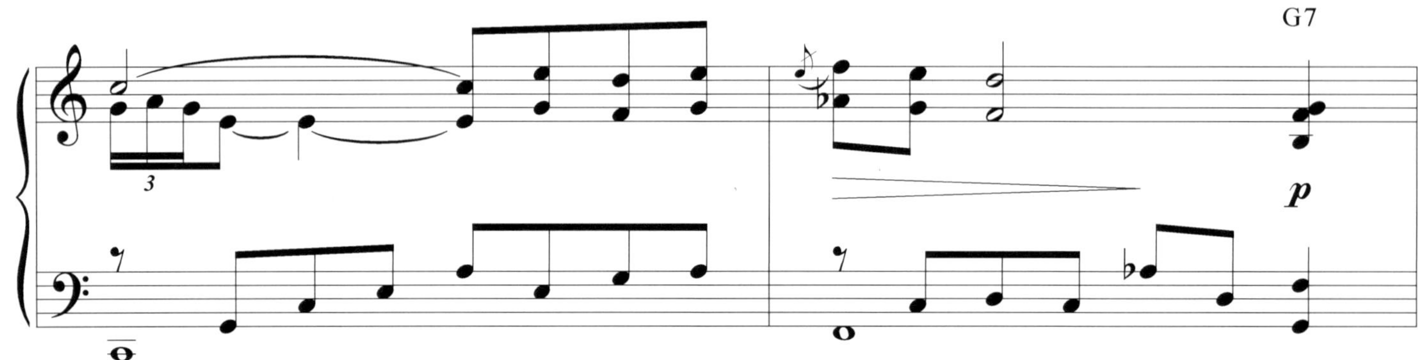

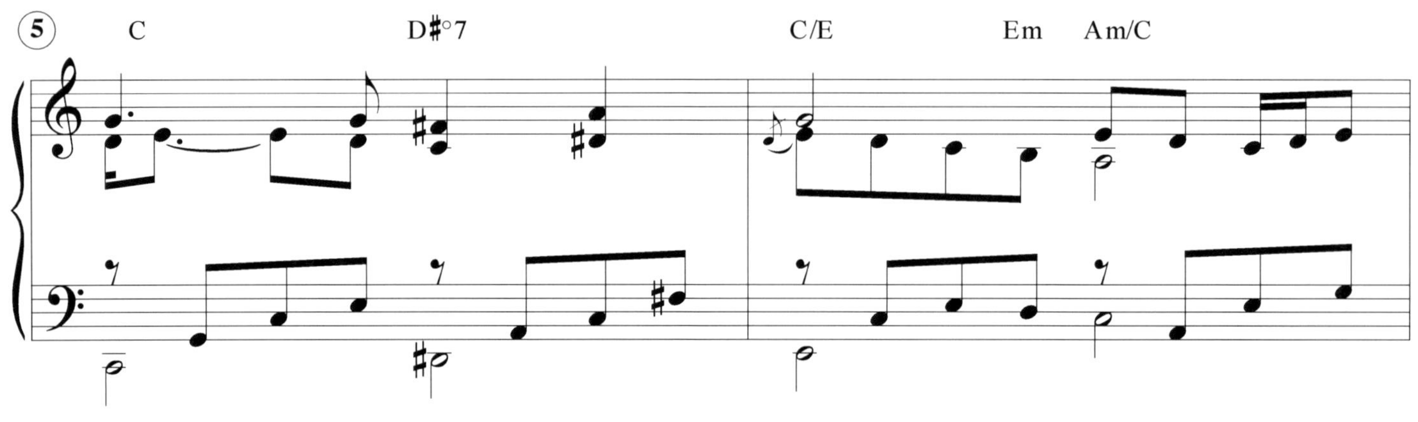

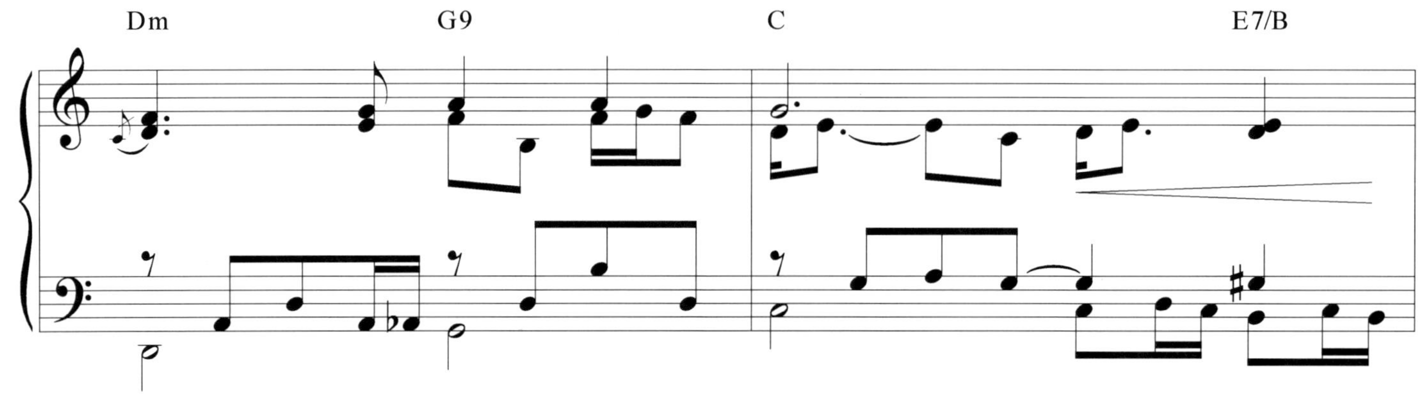

9
Am
E7/G♯
Am
C♯°7
Dm
Am
Dm/F
C°7
A°7
mf
poco a poco dim.
p
E/G♯
E7
E/D
13
C
G7
C
G7/D
mp
C
G/B
C
Gm/B♭
A7
cresc.
mf
Dm
Dm/A
Fm/A♭
17
G
G7
C6
C

C7
Fm
C/G
G7/B
C
C/G
C
Rhythm Tacet
mp
mf
22
3
26
f
B♭7
30
E♭
B♭7

E♭ B♭7/F E♭/G E♭7 C/E C/G C/E Fm Fm/C
34
B♭ B♭7 E♭6 E♭ E♭7 A♭m
E♭/B♭ G7/D
38
Cm Fm7(♭5) E♭ Cm
Fm9 B♭9 C C°7 C

Christ the Lord Is Risen Today

Lyra Davidica
Charles Wesley
Arr. Darrell V. Archer

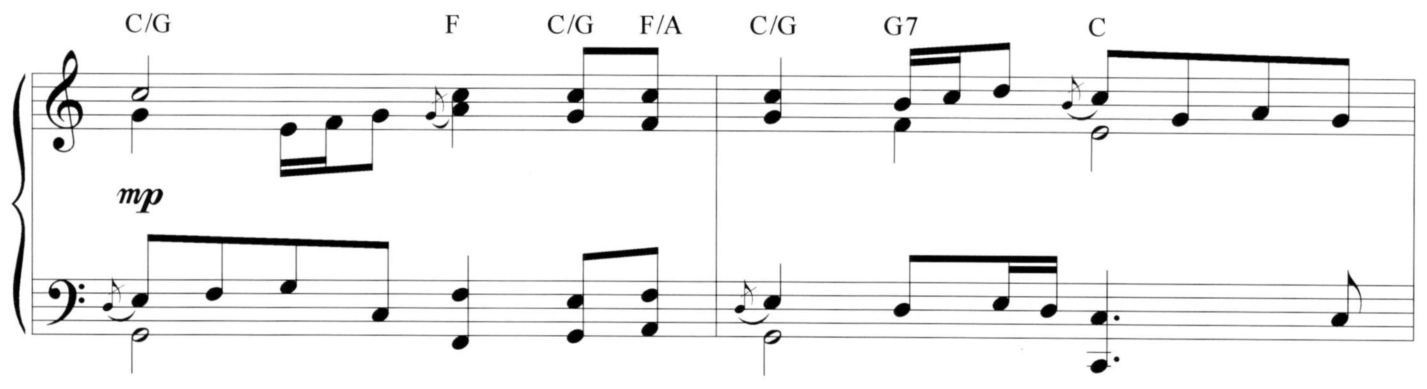
C/G
F
C/G
F/A
C/G
G7
C
mp

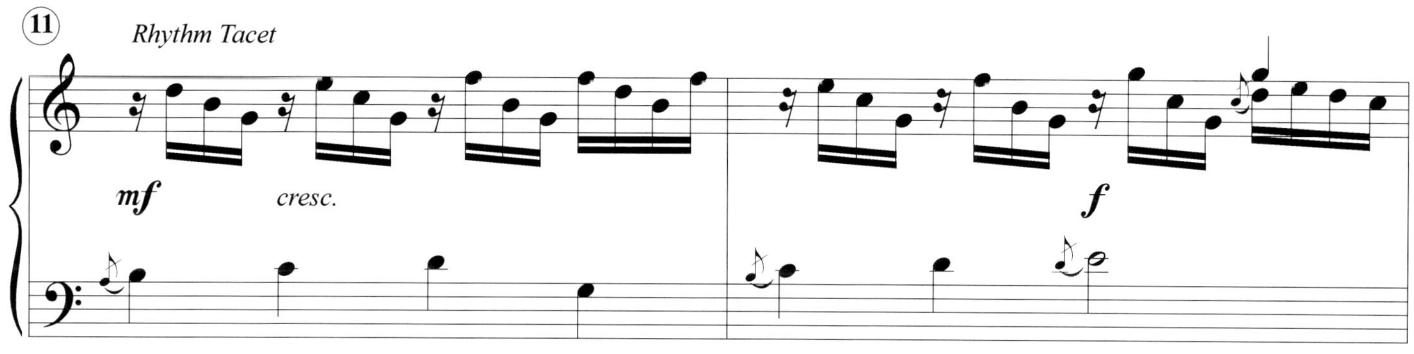
11
Rhythm Tacet
mf
cresc.
f

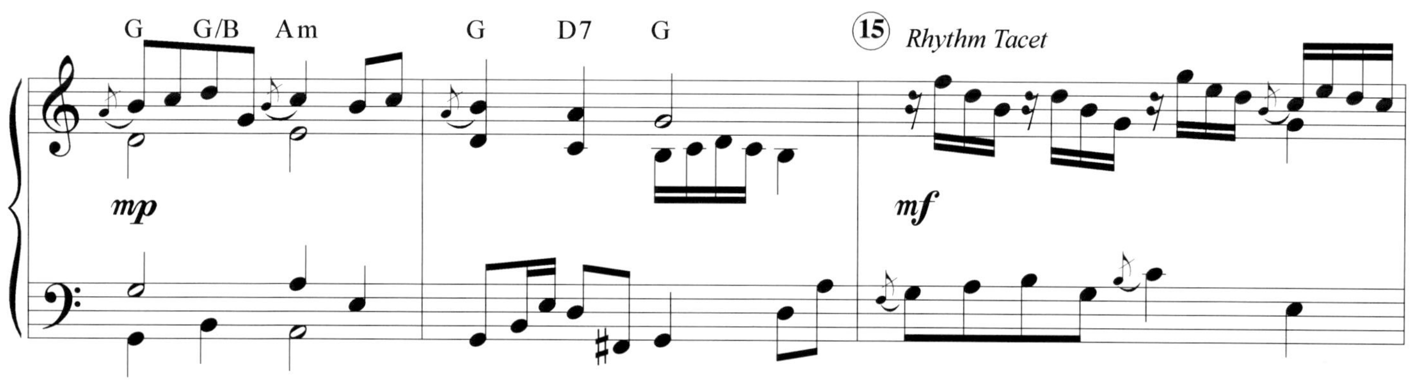
G
G/B
Am
G
D7
G
15
Rhythm Tacet
mp
mf

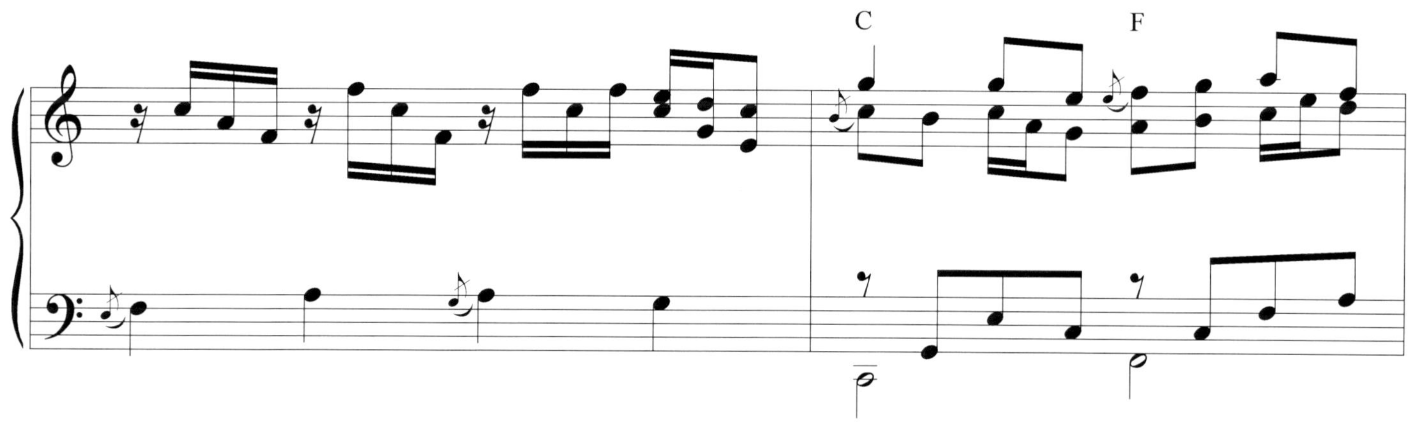
C
F

C/G
G7
C7
19
F
F/C
F
F7
f
B♭
F
B♭
F
C7
F
23
B♭
F
B♭
F
C7
F
B♭

F
C7
F
27
C
G7
C/E
/D
C7
8va
F/A
C/G
F
C
G7sus
G
C
F/A
mp
C/G
G7
C
31
C7
F
F7
f
B♭
F/A
B♭
mf

F/A
E°
F
35
B♭
f
C7
B♭
Am
3
Gm
Gm7/D
C7sus
C7
39
F
F7
mf
3
B♭
B♭/F
F
molto rit.

There Is a Fountain

Traditional American Melody Arr. Lowell Mason
Arr. Darrell V. Archer

William Cowper

C
C/E
F/A
Fm/A♭
13
C/G
Dm
Em/G
3
C
F
C/G
Dm/A
C
C/G
17
C
C/G
C
Am/E
f
Gm
C7
F
F/C
F
F/C
F
F/C
F
21
C/E
C
C/G
F
C/E
Am

D
D/F
G7
dim.
mf
3
25
C
Dm7
C/E
E+
8va
F6
Dm7
(8va)
C
C/E
F/A
Fm/A♭
29
C/G
Dm
Em/G
C
F
C/G
Dm/A

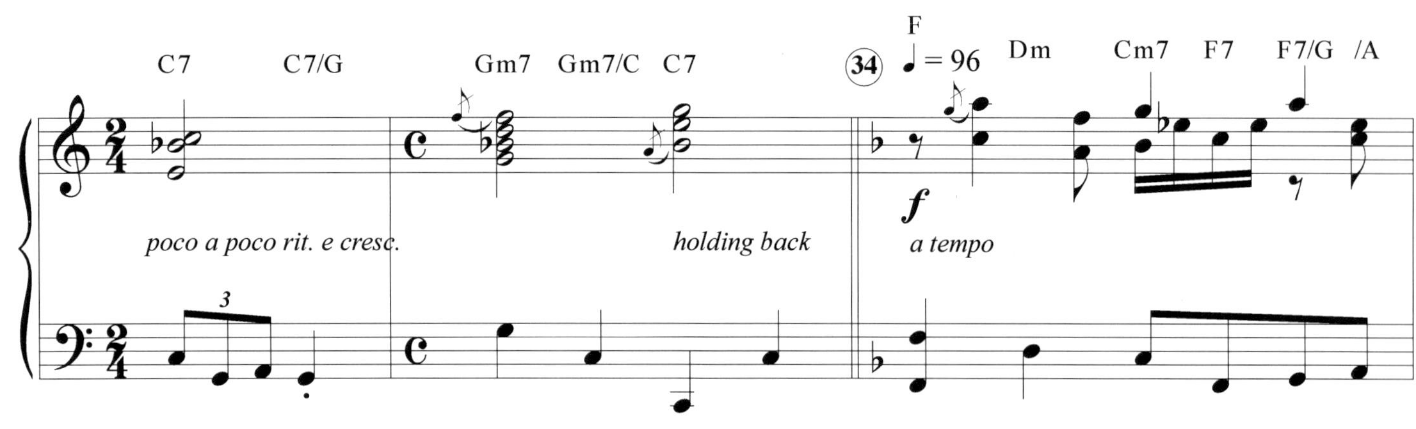
C7
C7/G
Gm7
Gm7/C
C7
34
F
♩= 96
Dm
Cm7
F7
F7/G
/A
3
poco a poco rit. e cresc.
holding back
f
a tempo

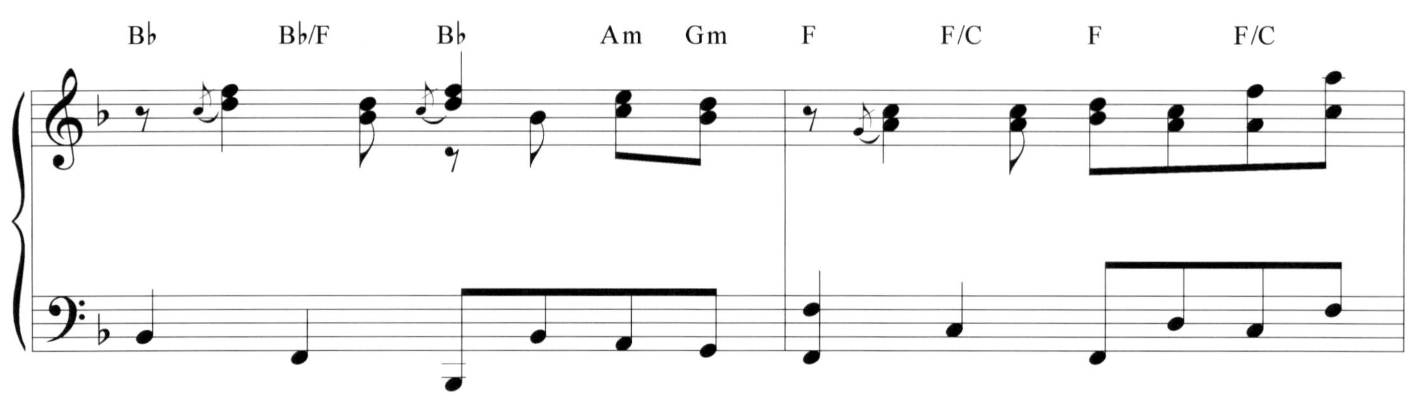
B♭
B♭/F
B♭
Am
Gm
F
F/C
F
F/C

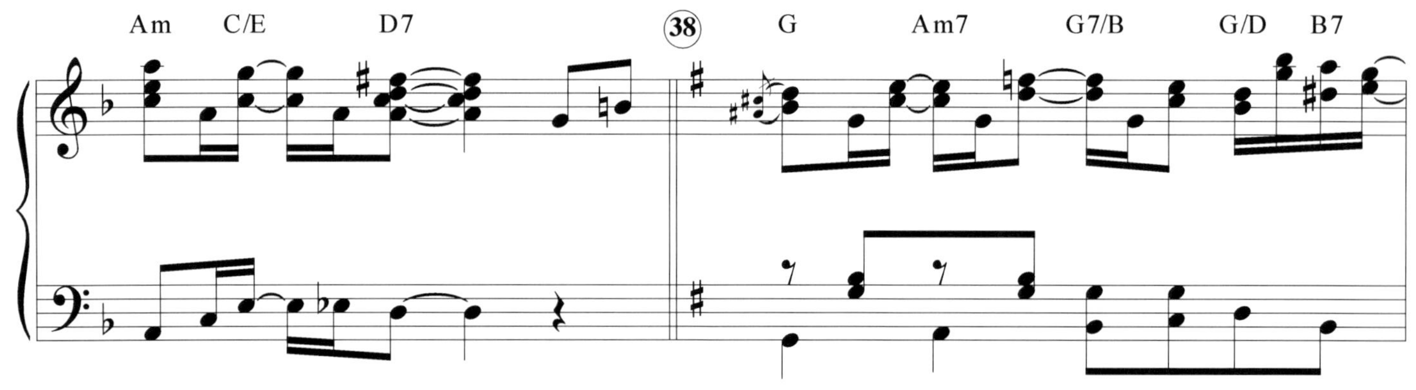
Am
C/E
D7
38
G
Am7
G7/B
G/D
B7

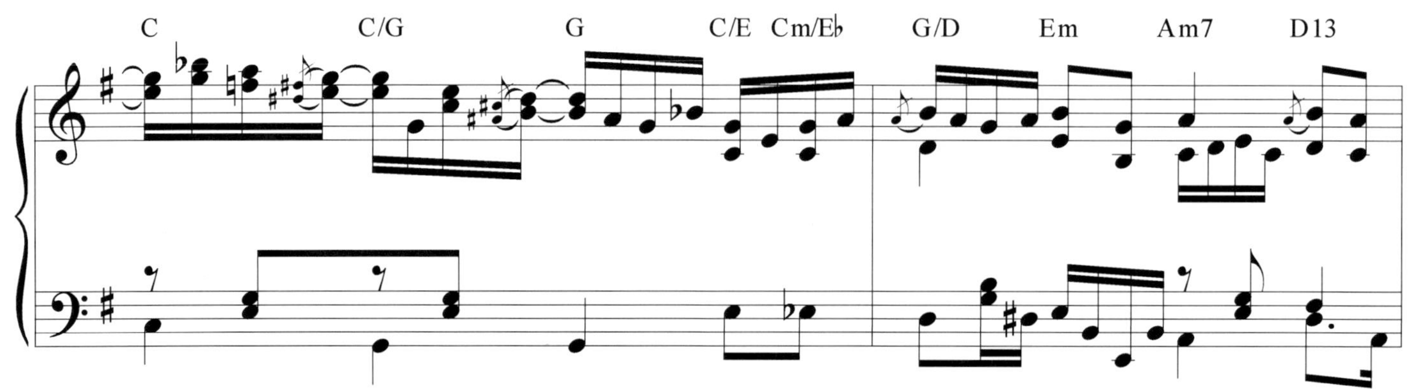
C
C/G
G
C/E
Cm/E♭
G/D
Em
Am7
D13

G
G7/B
C7
C7/G
42
G
G7/B
C7
C9/G
G
G7/B
C7
C/E
Cm/E♭
G/D
Em
Am7
D13
G
8va
no rit.
G7

Crown Him With Many Crowns

George J. Elvey
Arr. Darrell V. Archer

Brides - Thring

12
D
A7/E
D/F♯
G
G/F♯
Em7
B7/D♯
E
B7
E7
mf
A
A/G
A/F♯
A7/E
16
D
G
D/F♯
Em7
A7
f
dim.
D
D7
G
G△/E
Em7/A
A7
20
D
D/A
D6
D/A
mp
mf
C
C/G
D
E
E/B
E6
E/B
D
D/A
E

24
E
mf
A
E
Esus
E
f
D
C
B
28
E
A
E
F#
F#7
B
F#7
B
E
F#sus
F#7
B
C#m
B
D7
32
G
D7
G7
mp

C
E7
A
E7
A7
mf
D
Am6
D
D7
36
G
C
G/B
Am7
D7
f
G
G7
C
C△/A
Am7/D
D7
40
G
G/D
G6
G/D
mf
F
F/C
G
G
G/D
G6
G/D
F
F/C
G
f
ff

In the Cross of Christ I Glory

John Bowring

Ithamar Conkey
Arr. Darrell V. Archer

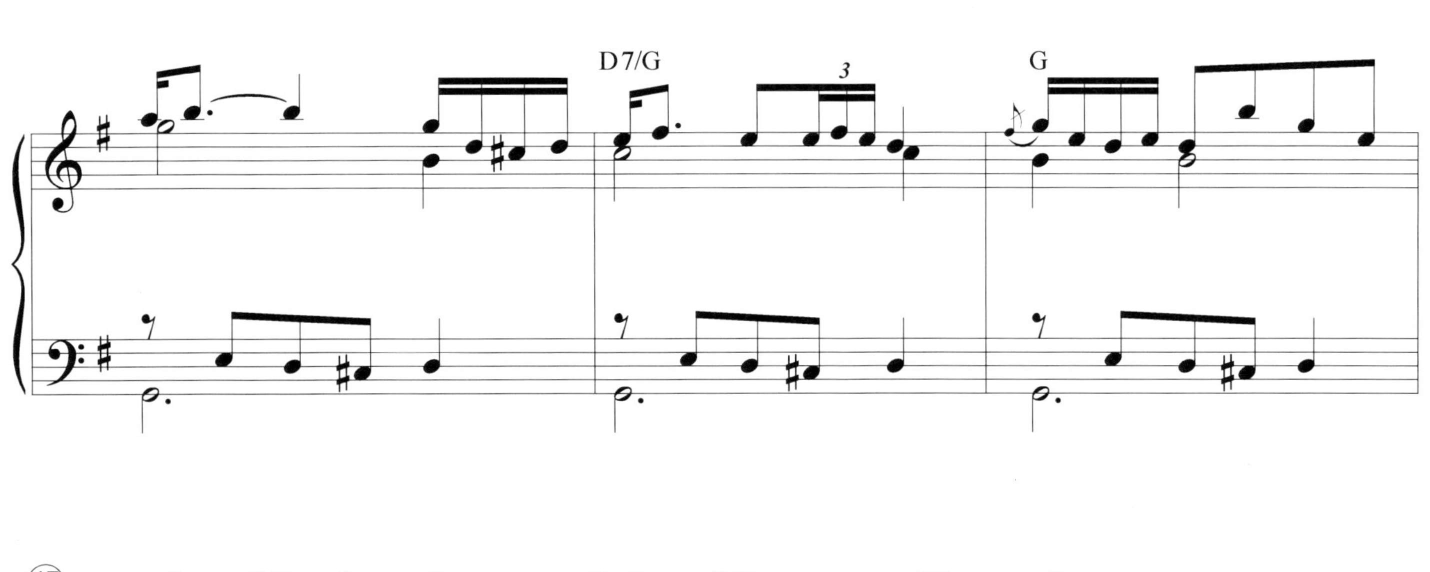
D7/G
3
G

17
G
G/D
C
G
Em7
G/D
D7
G
3

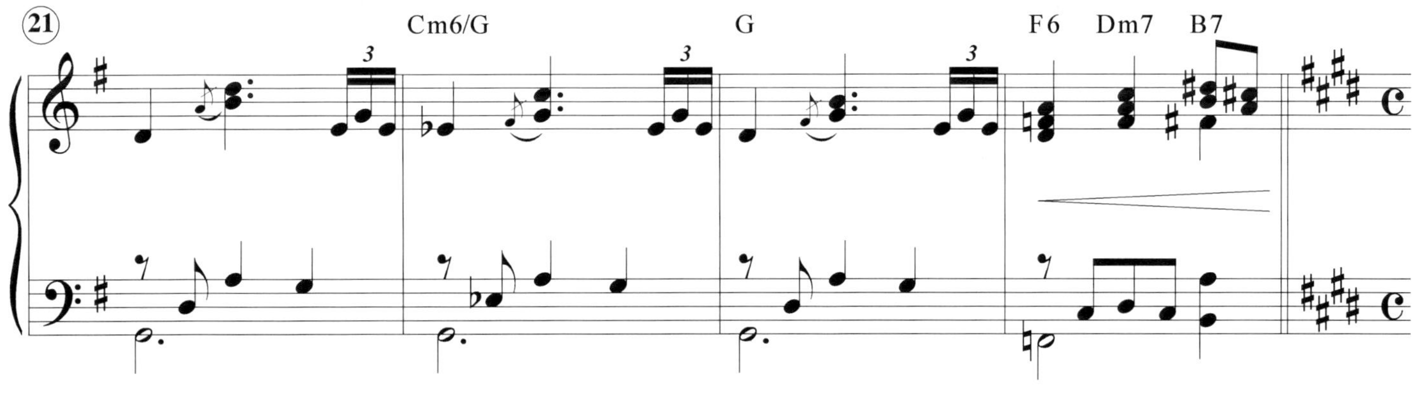
21
Cm6/G
3
3
G
3
F6
Dm7
B7

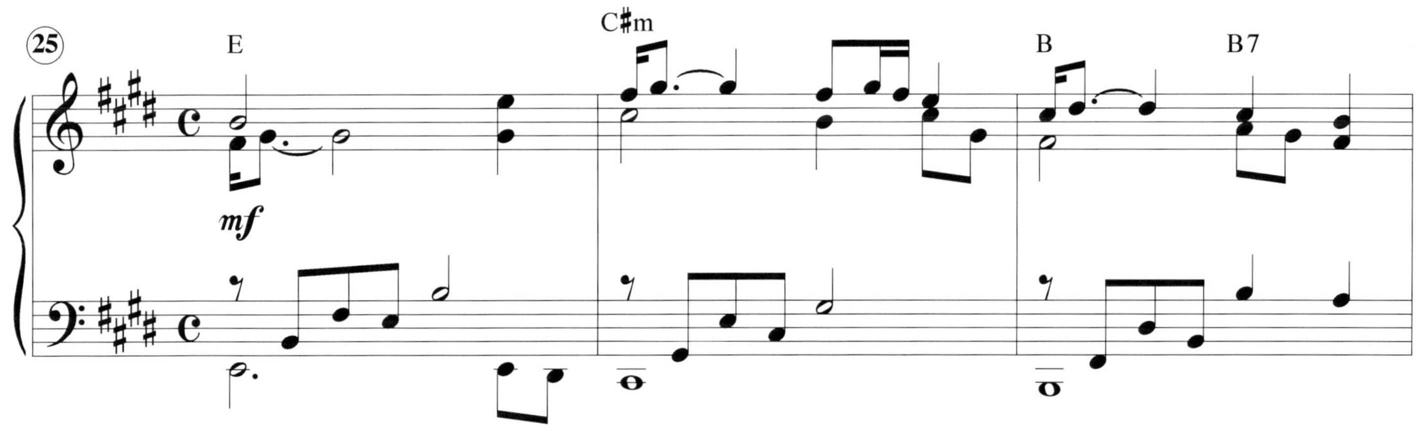
25
E
C♯m
B
B7
mf

E
29
F♯m7
G♯m
B7
E
F♯
B sus
B7
C7
33
F
f
C
B♭
C7
dim.
F
37
F
F/C
B6
F
Dm7
mp

F
C
F
mf
dim.
3
41
B♭m6/F
F
mp
B♭m/F
45
F
p
C7/F
F
poco a poco rit.

The Old Rugged Cross

George Bernard
Arr. Darrell V. Archer

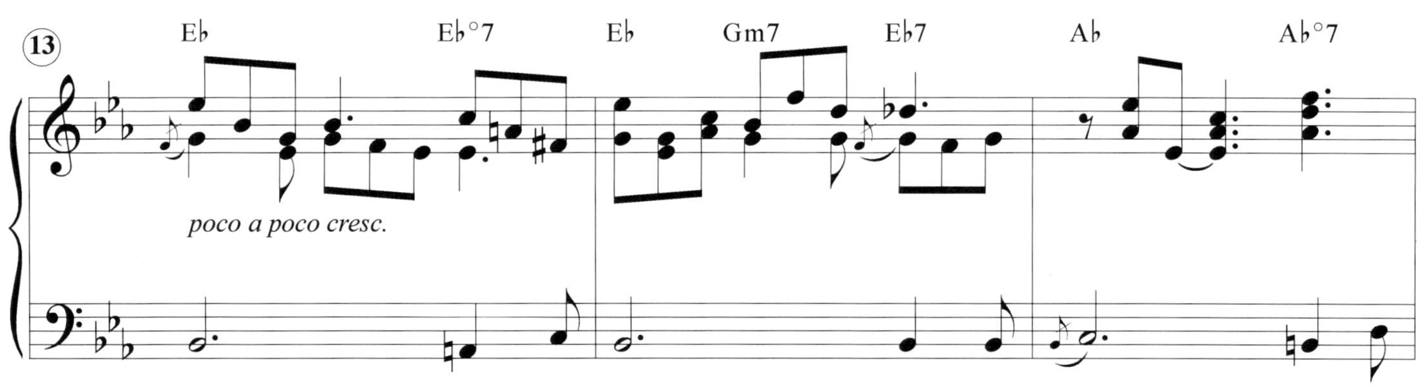
13
E♭
E♭°7
E♭
Gm7
E♭7
A♭
A♭°7
poco a poco cresc.

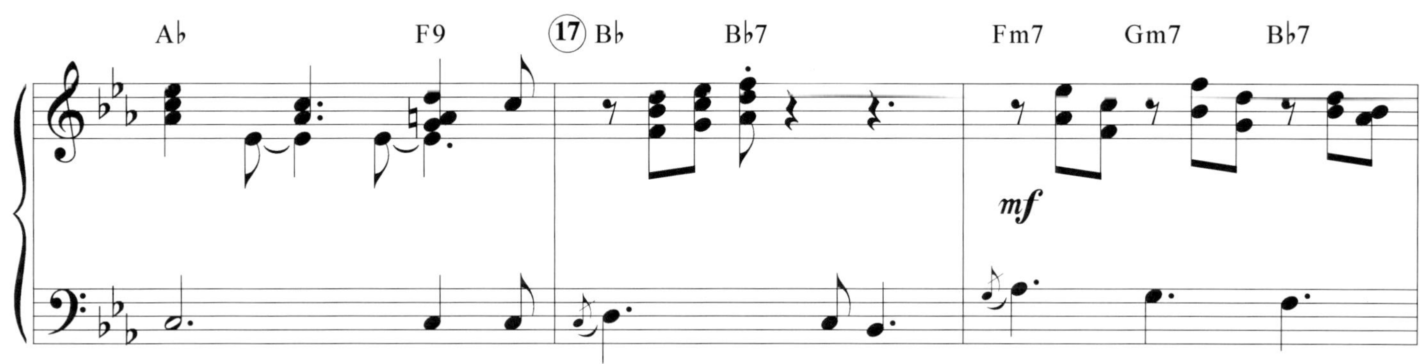
A♭
F9
17
B♭
B♭7
Fm7
Gm7
B♭7
mf

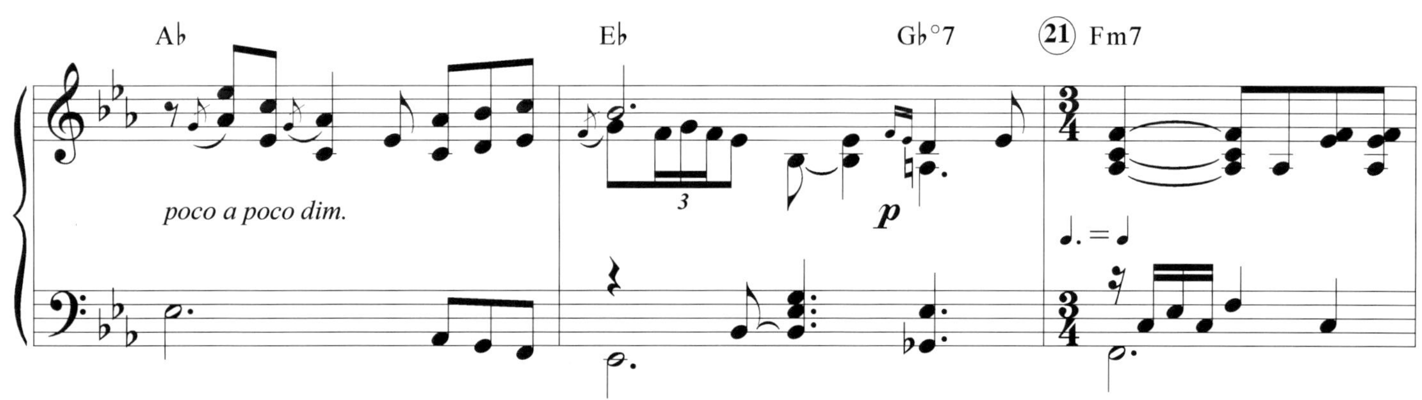
A♭
E♭
G♭°7
21
Fm7
poco a poco dim.
3
p
3
4

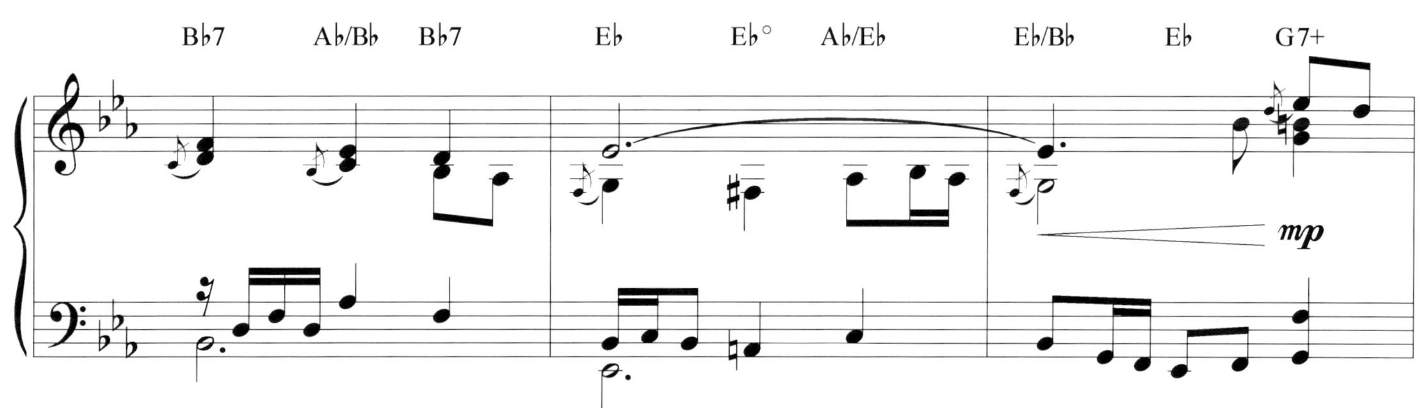
B♭7
A♭/B♭
B♭7
E♭
E♭°
A♭/E♭
E♭/B♭
E♭
G7+
mp

25
A♭
Gm
Fm
E♭
3
3
3
B♭
B♭7
Gm/B♭
Fm7/B♭
29
E♭
Gm7
B♭m6
B♭m7
E♭7
mf
A♭
Fm7
A♭m
33
E♭
E♭/B♭
mp
B♭
B♭7
E♭
G7
mf

37
Rhythm Tacet
D9
41
45
mp
poco a poco cresc.

49
f
Ab°7
53
Gm7
C7
Bb/C
C7
dim.
p
F
F°
Bb/F
F/C
F
A7+
57
Bb
mf
Am
Gm
F
Ab7sus
Ab7
Ebm7/Ab

61
D♭
D♭△
D♭7/F
D♭7sus/F
F+
G♭
G♭6
Fm
f
dim.
E♭m
G♭m
65
D♭
E♭m
D♭
mp
rall.
ff
A♭7sus
A♭7
G♭
Fm E♭m
f
poco a poco rit. e dim.
D♭
p

There Is Power in the Blood

Lewis E. Jones
Arr. Darrell V. Archer

G
G/D
G7
F/A
G7
C
(N.C.)
f
11
C
C/G
C
C/D
/E
F
F/C
C
Em
E♭°7
Dm
G
F/A
G7/B
C
(N.C.)
C
C/G
C
C/D
/E
F
F/C
C
Em
E♭°7

Dm
Dm7
Em/G
G7/B
C
F
C/E
Dm7

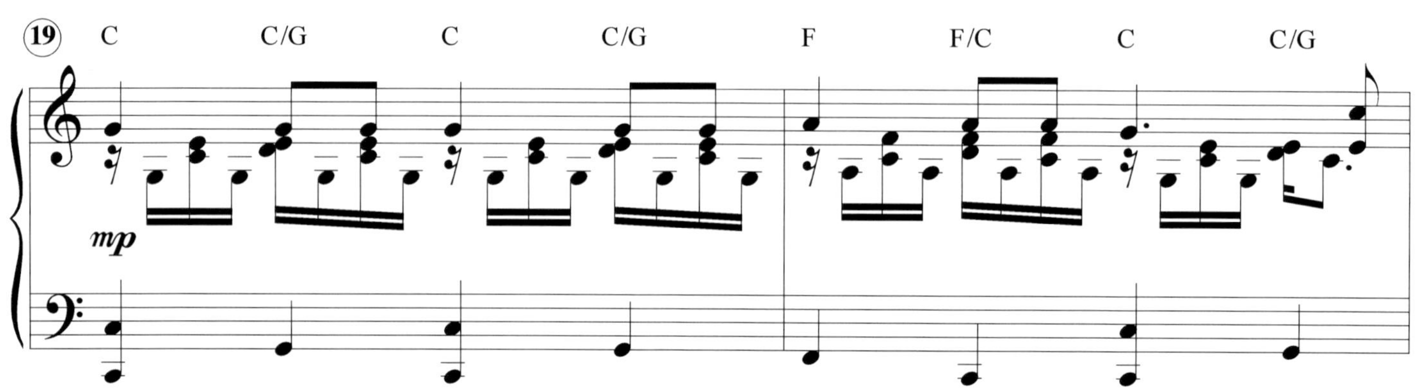
19
C
C/G
C
C/G
F
F/C
C
C/G
mp

G
Dm
G7
C
C/G
C

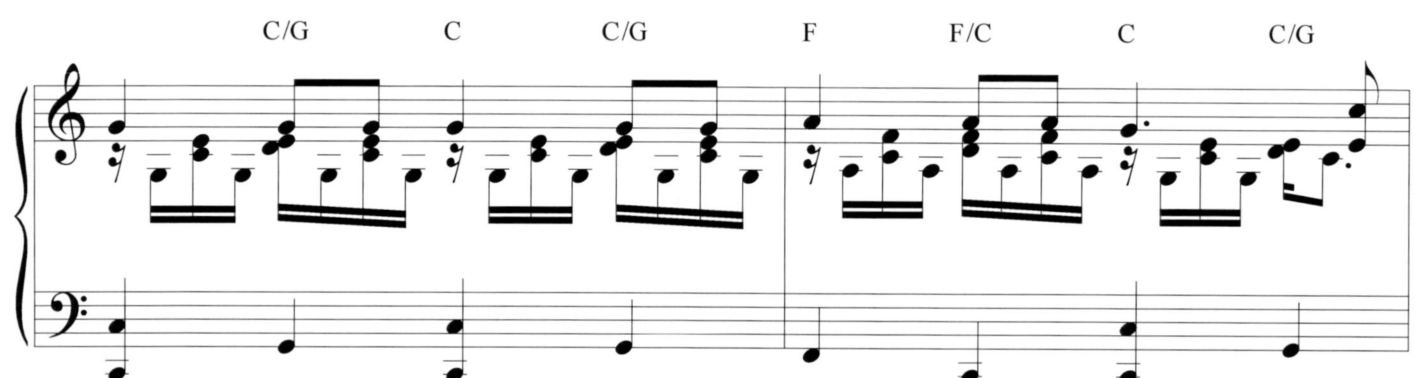
C/G
C
C/G
F
F/C
C
C/G

G7
G7/D
G7
F/G
G7
C
A♭
27
D♭
D♭/A♭
D♭
D♭/A♭
D♭△(♭5)/G
G♭
G♭/D♭
D♭
Fm
A7/E
mf
E♭m7
E♭m7/B♭
A♭
G♭/B♭
A♭7/C
D♭
D♭/A♭
D♭
D♭/A♭
D♭
D♭/A♭
D♭△(♭5)/G
G♭
G♭/D♭
D♭
Fm
A7/E

E♭m7
E♮m7/B♭
D♭/A♭
E♭m/B♭
A♭7/C
D♭
Bm7(♭5)/A
35
D
D/A
D
D/E
D7/F♯
f
G
G7/D
D
3
A
G
A7
D
B♭7

39
E♭
E♭/B♭
E♭
E♭/F
E♭7/G
ff
A♭
A♭7/E♭
E♭
Gm
G♭°7
Fm
E♭/B♭
B♭7/D
E♭
Cm
Fm7
E♭/B♭
B♭7
E♭
15ma
8va

Near the Cross

G+
B7
C
C/G
C
C♯°7
17
G/D
G
Em
Am
D7
to 𝄌
G
G/D
21
G
Bm
G9
G7
mp
C
C/G
C
25
G/B
C

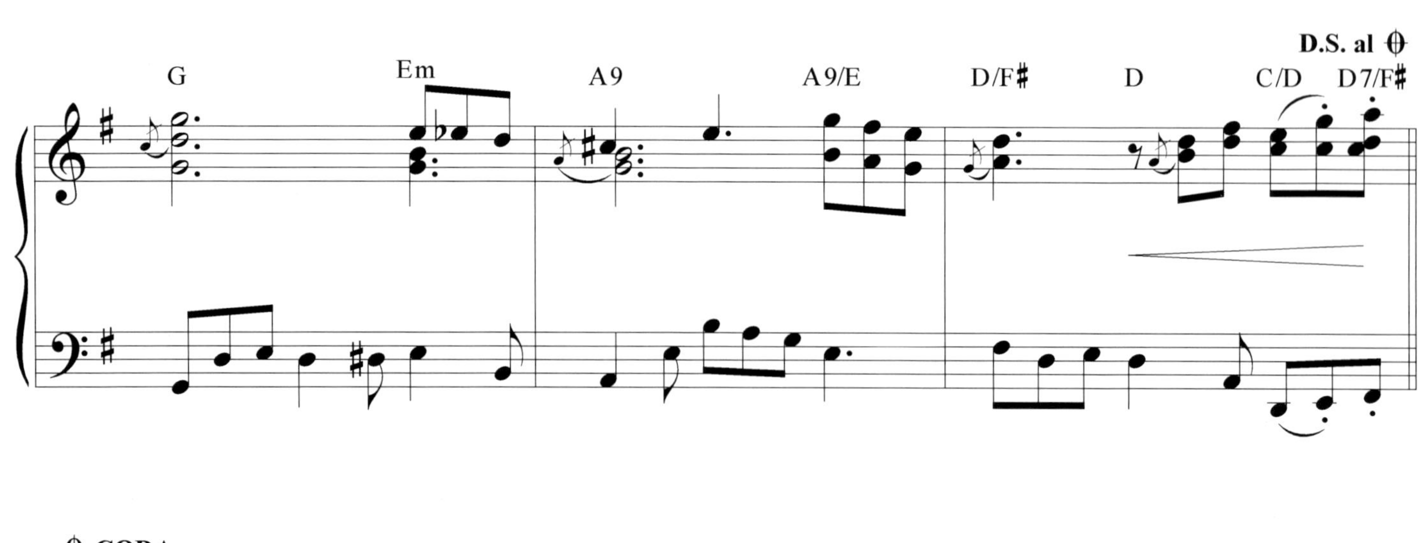
D.S. al 𝄌
G
Em
A9
A9/E
D/F♯
D
C/D
D7/F♯

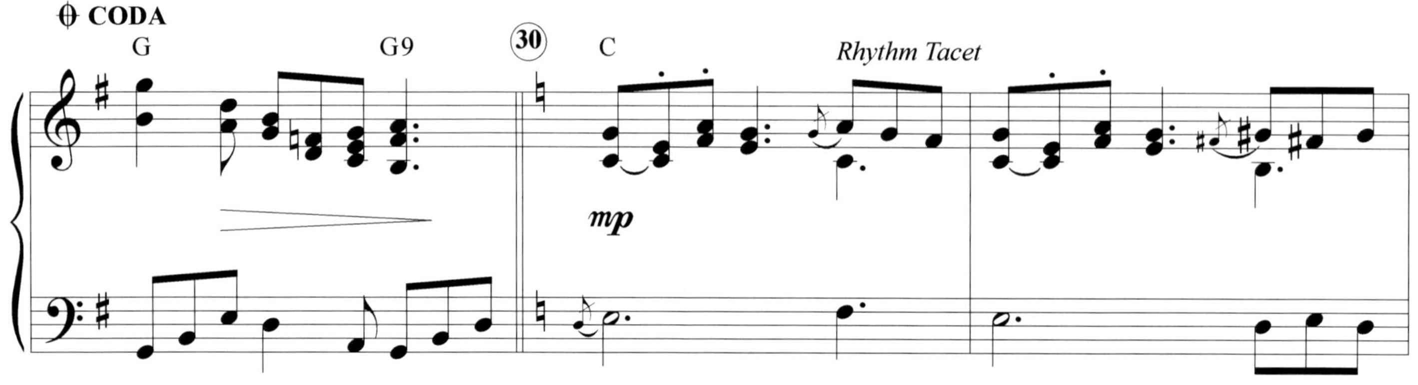
𝄌 CODA
G
G9
30
C
Rhythm Tacet
mp

34

G7

38
C
F/C
C+
E7
F
F♯°7
42
C/E
C/G
C
Am
(♮)

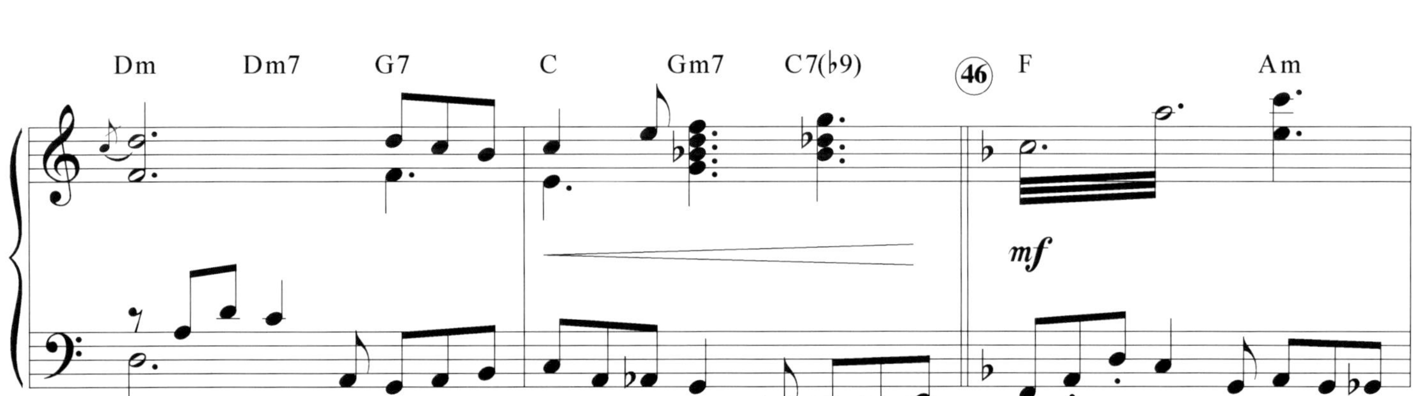
Dm
Dm7
G7
C
Gm7
C7(♭9)
46
F
Am
mf

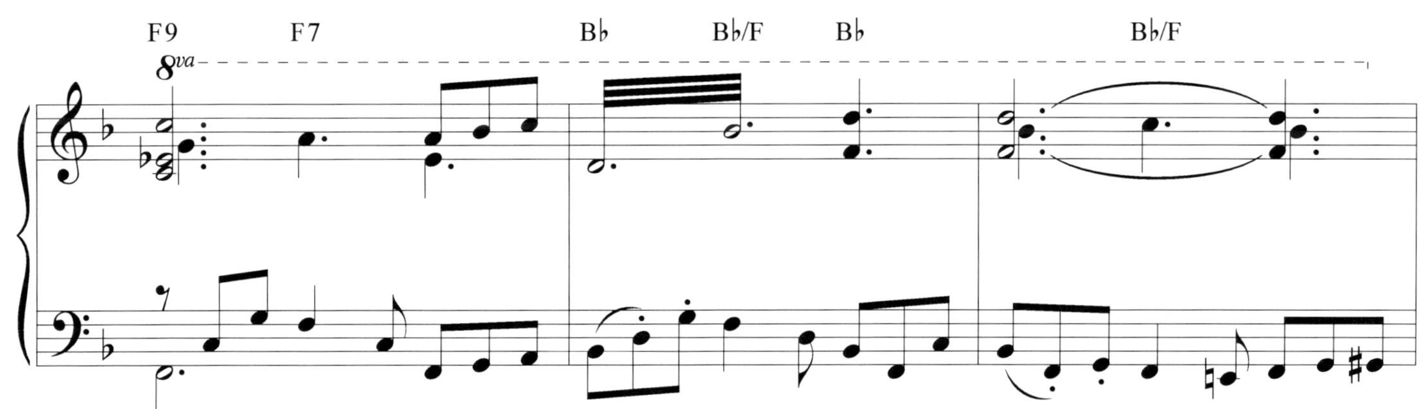
F9
F7
B♭
B♭/F
B♭
B♭/F
8va

50
F/A
B♭
F
Dm
G9
E♭7
D♭/E♭
E♭7
54
A♭
D♭
f
C+
C7/G
C7
D♭
dim.
mf
A♭°7
D°7
poco a poco rit. e cresc.
ff

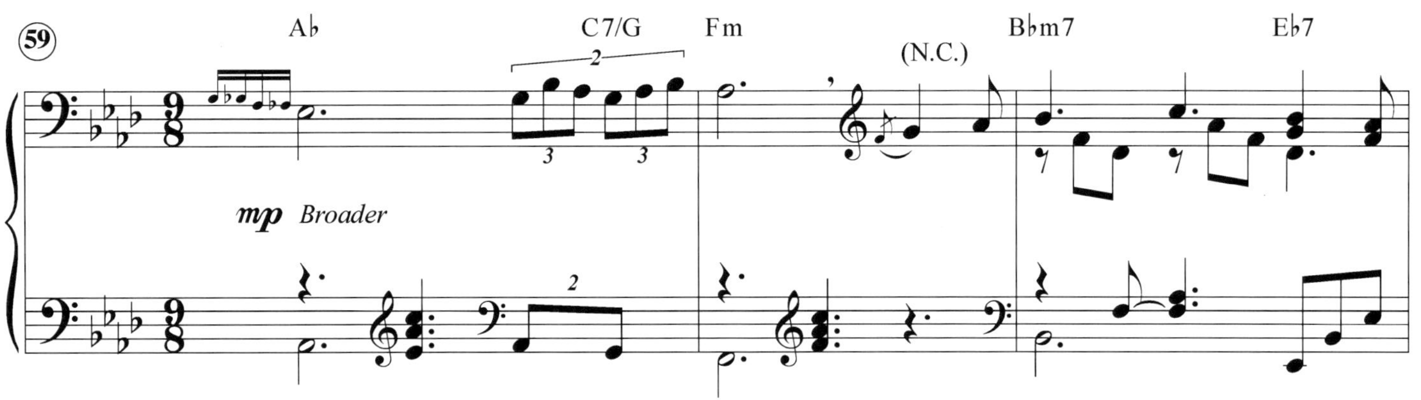

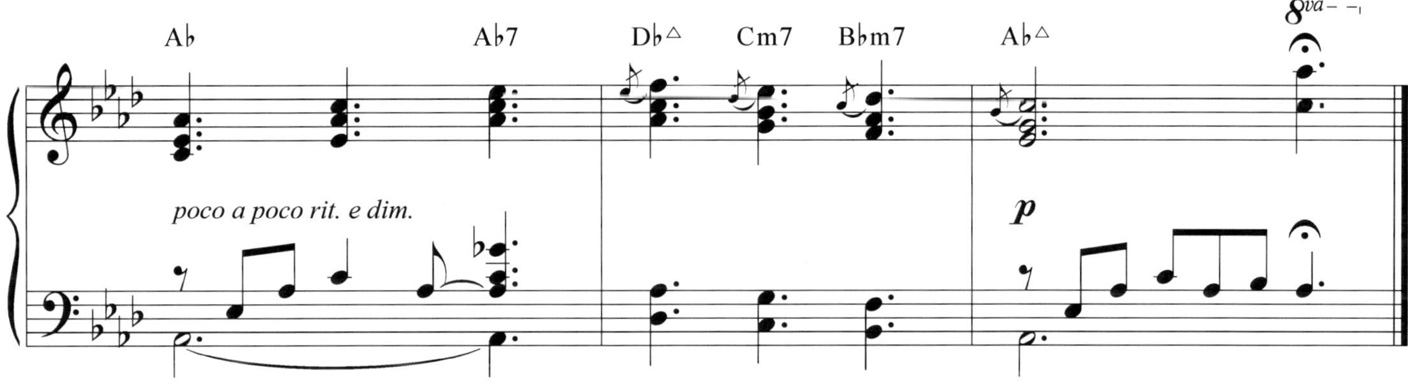

Jesus said to her,

" I am the **RESURRECTION** and the **LIFE**.

Whoever **Believes** in me, though he **DIE** yet shall he **Live**,

and everyone who lives and believes in me shall never die.
Do you believe this? "

John 11:25, 26

Other Mel Bay Sacred Piano Books

10 Gospel Favorites for Piano Solo (Archer)

12 Spirituals for Piano Solo (Gail Smith)

A Classic Christmas for Piano (Gail Smith)

A Country Piano Christmas (Archer)

Christian Classics for Piano Solo (Gail Smith)

Christmas Carols for Easy Piano (Benedict)

Christmas Carols for Piano Made Easy (Gail Smith)

Classical Piano for Worship Settings (Gail Smith)

Complete Church Pianist (Gail Smith)

Country Gospel Piano Solos (Gail Smith)

Easy Piano Solos for Worship (Shirley)

Easy Way Christmas Song Folio/Piano (S. Banks)

English Carols for Piano Solo (Gail Smith)

Favorite Hymns for Piano Solo (T. Price)

Favorite Hymns to Play for Piano (Leytham)

Gospel Piano Made Easy (Gail Smith)

Hymns Made Easy for Piano Book 1 (Gail Smith)

Hymns Made Easy for Piano Book 2 (Gail Smith)

Hymns Made Easy for Piano Book 3 (Gail Smith)

If Snowmen Could Make Music (Benedict)

Music is for Everyone Christmas Book Level 1 (Gilbert)

Old-Time Gospel Piano (Cummings/Whitmire)

Praise Piano Made Easy (Gail Smith)

Preludes and Offertories for Piano Solo (Gail Smith)

Wedding Music for Piano (T. Price)

WWW.MELBAY.COM